The Light of
My Reflection

Heyward Pearson

I0622781

Heyward Pearson Books

South Carolina

In Loving Memory of my sister Darlene Snoddy

Preface

I decided to write a book to give my children and grandchildren an idea of how I grew up and to be able to retell the challenges we've faced as a family while I still have some memory of them. This book is a series of short stories, taking place in the South, with each story peeling back layers of traumas from my childhood and layers of disappointments, betrayals, and prejudices that I faced later in life. While this book is non-fiction, the characters' names have been changed to give dignity to those involved in my upbringing. In writing this book, I've uncovered feelings and emotions that I have buried for years and have finally been able to find a way to discuss them aloud. I made many mistakes growing up, as I know many people have, but my goal for this book is that readers will discover that there is a light at the end of the tunnel. I want readers to understand that you will be tested in life, and the best thing you can do is trust in the Lord. To those who are struggling with family issues or facing the hard truths of the past, my hope is that you gain courage and keep pressing forward after reading these chapters. Lastly, to my children and grandchildren, I hope this book inspires you to make good decisions and to follow your dreams no matter what obstacles you may face.

Contents

Behind the Earl Taylor Peach Shed

As I watched Daddy's wrinkled hand tap the leather steering wheel of our car as his favorite song played over the radio, I should've known to keep my mouth shut. His station wagon bounced up and down on the road as we drove, dancing in sync to the beat. As we passed through one of the local neighborhoods, I saw a group of children playing soccer in the street. who stepped aside as we drove by. To my left sat my little brother Jamie, who held up his favorite toy airplane to the window and made rumbling noises to himself. I set my miniature Model T car on the dashboard and began maneuvering it back and forth, dreaming one day I'll own my own. Through the windshield, I felt the sun warming my forehead and cheeks. As we grew closer to the friend's house, Daddy insisted on stopping by be- fore dinner. He wore his usual shirt and blue jeans, but I could smell fresh cologne on him. He pulled his car into the driveway and then looked at my brother and I.

"Go play, boys. I'll be back soon," he said.

We both nodded and got out of the car as Daddy did the same, closed the door, and left us alone to play with the other kids out front. Out of the corner of my eye, I watched him as he walked up the sidewalk to the front door, stepped past a bicycle leaning against one of the bushes, and knocked on the front door of the house I had never seen before. The house stood two stories tall, much larger than our little shack behind the cotton fields. The door opened, and a woman peaked out at him and then let him slip inside the house. I didn't think anything of it at that age, so I played basketball with my brother and the other children in the driveway.

About 30 minutes later, Daddy appeared outside the woman's house once more. Daddy's friend, wearing a silky robe, stood in the doorway and winked at him as he waved goodbye. He made his way over to the driver's side of the car with a smile on his face and told us to come on, and the three of us hopped inside the station wagon. He started the car and backed out of the driveway, not telling either of us how his meeting went and why he needed to stop here with such urgency. It took about twenty minutes for us to get home, and because I knew the streets of Duncan well, it didn't take me long to remember the way to get back there again. When Daddy pulled up on to our gravel driveway and parked, my brother and I hopped out of the car and joined Darlene, Doris, Lena, and Linda in the front yard. Daddy went inside to where Mama stood in the kitchen while making dinner.

I heard Mama's voice ring out from the kitchen as he greeted her and moved inside. Even from out here, I smelled something delicious cooking. When Mama wasn't in the house, she often went out back and worked in the barn behind the shack. She raised pigs, so when they grew nice and plump, she would slaughter them, salt the meat, and then hang the meat to purify. Then she'd draw some water from the well in our backyard and wash her hands. Because of her hard work, we often ate ham, pork chips, and various other cuts of the pig. Other times, she would work in the garden and harvest sweet potatoes in order to make her delicious pies. Arriving home, I found my sister Darlene counting aloud with her eyes closed against the tree while the others hid in the area. We waited to join the next round. I looked around the area and tried to decide whether to hide under our dark green house, within the mud of the pigpen, behind the pile of garden supplies, or inside the barn with the hanging meat. My sister ran off to start her searching while Jamie and I waited. Once she found my other siblings, we both joined in and played several rounds.

Sometime later, I went to count for the first time, but Mama came outside, looking dressed to impress as always, and she asked me, "Where did you and Daddy stop on your way home?"

I replied, "At his friend's house." "Can you show me where at?"

I nodded, as she directed me to join her in the station wagon once more, and I gave her directions road by road to the woman's house over in Wellford. We parked outside on the road once we arrived, and Mama stared out the window and watched the house with suspicious expectation. I didn't understand at the time why she had brought me back, but sometime later, the side door to the kitchen swung open. The woman from earlier gave a quick glance outside, and then, she pushed her son outside as he held a bag of trash. With a deep frown on his face, he carried it out to the metal can and placed it inside before scurrying back to the kitchen. I heard Mama huff before starting the car and driving home. The sun started to set as we returned to the house, and she wouldn't make eye contact with me at all. Her eyebrows remained furrowed the whole ride, up until the moment she stepped into the house where Daddy sat reading the paper, and then, her face slid back into its kind, neutral expression. Nothing out of the ordinary happened that night, but over the next couple of days, our family dynamic changed forever, and I knew that I had caused it.

My parents began to fight more often whenever they shared the same room, and whenever that happened, my siblings and I made sure to stay away and go outside. Often, Mama would hit Daddy or throw anything she could get her hands on at him, but he never acted with aggression beyond yelling back. In a way, I think Daddy knew that he brought her rage upon himself, and thus, he didn't fight back against her, even to defend himself. Once news got around about Daddy's cheating, many of Mama's friends told her to handle her situation and overcome it. As a strong, Christian woman, she knew doing anything drastic had the potential to destroy everything. She disregarded their concerns and instead drowned her worries in alcohol. She began drinking Vodka on a regular basis — so much so that Linda tried sneaking water into her drinks before giving them to Mama.

"Somebody tampered with my Vodka," she said.

Linda loved her enough to tell the truth, take the beating, and continue to add water to her alcohol in order to keep her safe.

Overtime, Mama's trust did not improve. She treated every woman her husband met as a threat. At one time, she believed that Daddy had a girlfriend who worked at Home Light with him. To make sure he didn't stare anywhere except the road in front of him, she always had a makeshift weapon in the passenger side door that she could hit him with if his eyes strayed. Sometimes, it would be a hammer, a set of pliers, or some scissors — whatever she could get her hands on. Daddy had his nose broken several times from their disputes of the years. Every time they got into in the car with us, we all sat there terrified, thinking Mama would injure Daddy. Once, she got so violent that when we pulled off onto the side of the road, we climbed out of the backseat and ran up a steep hill to avoid their conflict.

Once they calmed down, Mama stepped out of the car, put her hands on her hips, and yelled, "Ya'll get back in this car right now."

Fearing her wrath, we squished back inside the vehicle while Daddy held a rag to a fresh cut on his nose. Hearing their arguments made us fearful for their lives. We didn't want to lose either of them, and I think underneath it all, Mama and Daddy knew this.

Despite their frequent fighting in those days, we survived. Mama and Daddy stayed together for us children and for the sake of one day obtaining a better lifestyle for us all. The fact that my parents worked separate jobs during the day kept us together in the end, due to the pay as well as the fact that it kept them away from each other for a good part of the day. Mama would often take Daddy to work and then went to do her cafeteria job at my school. Daddy, on the other end, worked two jobs: one at Greenville Steel and the other at Greenville's Woodside Mill. He worked as a welder up until the day he had an accident. During one of his projects, a piece of steel fell and broke his leg. His injury left him out of work for six weeks, but

Mama stepped up to provide for the household. When she started working at the local chicken farm, she would come home each day in her apron and hair net and would bandage her cut up fingers. Together, my parents saved up their money in order to move us into a larger and safer house one day. In that goal, everyone agreed that we needed to upgrade.

The shack we lived in had many problems. For one, the house had no insulation, so we often slept in the cold. The place also had no foundation beyond some rocks, so often critters and insects would sneak their way into our home, to the utter disgust and fear of Mama and my sisters. This one time, a snake crawled in through a small hole in the wall. My siblings and I sat together at the kitchen table while Mama cooked dinner and Daddy read the paper. I saw the creature sneaking up behind Linda first and yelled out "snake" in warning, but my speech impediment led the rest of them to hear "lake." Time seemed to slow down as their eyes landed on the serpent slithering on the floor, and Daddy went to grab the shotgun. He came back with his finger holding the trigger and took aim.

He said, "Duck, sweetie."

As he did, he loosed a shot at the snake, blowing it to pieces and putting a massive hole in the wall. It took several seconds before the ringing in our ears subsided and the smoke cleared. We all stood there in silence and took in the gruesome scene and the even larger hole in the wall. Moments like these sharpened Mama's desire to move out as soon as possible.

When the day came, our family moved from the shack to a nicer house in Greer, South Carolina. It had one additional bedroom than we had before and a sturdy foundation, and it put Daddy closer to his work. The house sat behind the Earl Taylor Peach Shed, a local business that sold fruits and vegetables but specialized in peaches. The owner owned a lot of the land, and he let us rent one of the houses built on it. We established a comfortable life there. My siblings and our friends would often knick peaches from the fields near my house, but we found out that an evil bull guarded the produce. It chased us all for miles, and in the end, only some of us made it back home while the others climbed a pine tree until it wandered off. I never laughed so hard in my life that day. We also joined a new church called Rock Hill. My parents would often invite Pastor Chappel over for dinner, and my siblings and I stayed outside to show our respect.

Visits from the pastor or the move to a new house didn't stop my parents' fighting. It got bad enough that even when we visited other people's houses, they couldn't stop themselves. We had visited my uncle Bundt's house this one time, so he could cut all the men's hair. Mama and sisters came along as well and caught up with my Aunt Geraldine. I don't know what sparked her anger, but Mama all of a sudden stood up from her spot in the living room, began yelling at Daddy, and went to get her gun out of the car. My aunt jumped into action, retrieved her own gun, and wielded it against Mama before she could, while also pushing us outside and making sure that we got out of harm's way.

The sun had set already, so we all stood in the darkness with their porch light providing us the only light to see with. With her gun in hand, Mama froze. We could hear the sound of Mama's and our aunt's screams echoing inside. I can't remember who took off first, but we all dashed away from that house and began running through the fields of cotton. It had grown about four feet tall, so all of us stood above it as we ran through the crops without disturbing them. Once we got a decent distance away, we all sat down and disappeared in the sea of fluff. The six of us remained silent and frozen in place as we sat in darkness and dirt with no source of light within range to bring us comfort. We had gotten lost. At one point, the distant sound of a woman crying emanated nearby. We all remained motionless with fright and wondered if that was our Mama or some phantom.

No one spoke during this time, but we all wanted to ask, "Are Mama and Daddy okay?"

We should've asked, "Will we be okay?"

An hour passed with no change until we heard a car door open and close nearby before an engine roared to life and echoed across the fields. It sounded like the car drove closer to our position before we found ourselves blinded by the bright lights of our car. She yelled out our names, and upon hearing her anger, we all stood up and projected long shadows behind us as we ran over to her. As we all clambered into the backseat, neither Daddy nor Mama spoke on their way home. We could feel the intensity between them, despite their fighting having ended for now, but we dared not spark another.

As the years went on, we spent many years in this house, and my siblings and I grew into ourselves more. After school, some of us would go to Campabello and Dobinson's Farm to pick peaches. We would gather them into big boxes and load them on to a huge tractor trailer for $1.50 a box. This way, we earned some money to buy whatever we wanted without having to ask our parents for money. Mama let us take the job if we promised to still go to school every day. She cared about our educations. One day, my sisters Lena and Linda decided to ditch school for the day. They had $0.59 to spend and went shopping. They spent the whole day wandering around downtown Greer. My sisters, who hadn't gotten on the school bus that day, waited for me at the bus stop and tried to convince me to lie for them as we walked home. I kept my promise up until the point where Mama threatened to punish me if I lied. Both Linda and Lena took a beating, and they learned to never skip school again, or else Mama would find out.

Despite liking the house behind the peach shed, Mama felt dissatisfied with the life she provided us with. She dreamed of moving us into the city where we could live in better conditions and live closer to the stores. Even more so, she wanted to live in a house where she could watch her children could grow up and she could grow old. With dreams often come disappointments.

Within Spartanburg General Hospital

hen you don't have to worry about animals crawling into your house through the underpinning, you've found a good house. The place in question sported a pastel blue paint, had a white front porch to lounge on, and three bedrooms — Mama built an extra room to make sure we all fit. We still had to share the same restroom, which led the usual squabbles for mirror time or privacy. Daddy's international truck and Mama's big Cadillac often sat outside in the yard. Beside them, we stored our mini bikes, which my friends and I used to ride around the neighborhood. The fenced in yard provided plenty of space for us to play with the neighbors under Mama's supervision. For lack of a better phrase, we had it good. Daddy still worked the same jobs he had before with a shorter commute, and Mama continued to cook two of everything for when we would re- turn home from work and school each day. Mama even started teaching Darlene and Linda how to cook. She taught them how to make our favorites, from the fruity sweetness of blackberry pie and peach cobbler to the savory tastes of chicken dinners and chili dogs. During the first year, no one questioned Mama's reasoning for spending a considerable amount of time and effort passing on her knowledge and recipes to her two oldest daughters. We saw it as a rite of passage and moved on.

Life went on as usual with the occasional but violent fights between my parents and Mama's resulting increase in suspicion and drinking. While Mama often hosted friends and loved ones at our new home, she still showed caution when bringing other women around Daddy in fear his eyes or slick tongue would wander. While the adults spent time together, often the other kids and I would go play hide and seek. Other times, I would go play baseball and football in the nearby field with my cousins and neighbors. Back in that day, I had no muscle compared to other kids and weighed around 100 pounds, if that. I had speed and agility on my side but not much strength. One kid on the block weighed over 400 pounds, which made him impossible to tackle when he charged across the field for a touchdown. It often took three defenders to get him down, and due to my speed, I always reached him first. While I leaped on to his back and looped my arms around his neck, I put all my weight into the takedown.

"I've got him!"

The whale didn't fall until two more of my teammates landed on top of me. We collapsed into a dog pile on the patchy grass field, and I felt the air rush out of me. Even after the other kids climbed off and flipped me over, I laid there dazed, tried to catch my breath, and saw hypothetical stars. Several of my friends lifted me up by the belt buckle in order to help me recover. From that point on, I stuck with baseball.

When my siblings and I didn't find ourselves playing outside,

Mama would often have us follow our older sisters when they went out on dates with boys. Once, Darlene stayed out late and tried to sneak into the house without Mama knowing. All us kids knew that doing anything inappropriate in Mama's eyes led to punishment. We acted as her spies because our fear of her outweighed our fear of our sibling's reactions once they found out who snitched. Darlene came in to take a bath, and Mama waited up for her. There, in the bath- room, she punished her daughter for staying out late with a stranger and whooped her with a drop cord. Mama ran a tight ship and kept us in line with the threat of her temper. While we knew that she loved us, she didn't allow any nonsense in her household.

Mama even treated my friends like her own. Robbie, one of my best friends, came from an Indian family, and his mother Mrs. Mae had 12 children. Mama felt bad for her because she had lost 3 children in the past. Robbie, like the rest of his siblings, looked slim, and Mama made sure to feed him plenty whenever he'd come over. One night, Mrs. Mae showed up to our home in sheer panic.

She cried, "My baby ate some of the red devil lye, and he's dying!"

Between her panicked sobs, she explained how Robbie had wandered into the kitchen and rummaged through the pantry and cabinets. He somehow got his hands on the container of Red Devil Lye and began to eat some of the white crystalline powder. Mama explained to us later that adults used that chemical for cleaning the sink drain, not for cleaning out a throat canal. The second the sodium hydroxide started dissolving in his saliva, it began to burn the inside of his mouth and throat. Upon hearing his cries and seeing the open container on the counter, Mrs. Mae rushed over to our house, banged on our front door, and begged Mama and Daddy to come quick so that they could take Robbie to the hospital.

"Stay here and behave. Darlene, you're in charge," Mama said. In the fearful silence of the house after the family car sped away,

I asked Darlene, "Will Robbie be okay?"

I can't remember her exact reply, but she said something comforting like, "He'll be okay, Heyward."

As I laid in bed that night, I could imagine my Daddy scooping Robbie up, putting him in the back seat, and then speeding to Spartanburg General's emergency room. I learned after that my friend passed out in his Mama's lap during the drive. The moment they arrived, a doctor and several nurses loaded Robbie onto a gurney and rushed him away. Looking back on the moment, I felt relieved that I didn't have to see the pain on Robbie's face nor hear his hysterical wailing because I doubt that I would've forgotten it easily. We found out after Robbie's surgery that if my parents had gotten him there any later Robbie would have died. He ended up with a long scar on the side of his neck where the doctors had to cut open his throat and treat his burns. Despite his near-death experience, everyone on the block and at school thought he was the coolest kid around. Mama, on the other hand, watched him like a hawk every time he came over after that point.

Mama often had friends and family over when she could. She would invite her brother, his girlfriend, and his kids over for dinner. Doing so allowed her to catch up on their lives and keep them close for support. All us kids would play games outside, and the adult would sit on the front porch and drink their worries away. While my parents liked to socialize at home, they would, on occasion, go out. They frequented the same club in Lyman and went there to drink and let loose for the night. Mama would often come up with idea, and Daddy would go with her to make sure that she didn't get into any trouble. As I got older, I knew that she went there to get back at him for cheating on her. None of us kids ever went inside the club to witness our Mama's partying, but remembering how most of their nights out ended in a fight and a silent drive home, I imagine her flirting didn't look good. During these times, we never had a babysitter to watch us, so my parents brought us along and made us wait in the car. My parents always put Darlene in charge in these situations because she was the oldest. She sat up front and kept an eye on the outside of the car while the rest of us all remained squished into the back seat. We brought toys along with us or played games in the car to pass the time, like I Spy. From behind glass windows, we watched as drunken people stumbled out of the club and found their cars. Only a few adults ever noticed us, but we did get some stares and nasty looks.

One by one, we each fell asleep either against the doors or on one another. We'd wake up when our parents would exit the club, mid fight, slam the doors shut in anger, and force Darlene to sit between them.

Daddy asked, "Why do you always rub it in my face? I told you I'd not do it again!"

Mama replied, "I like to have fun. I can do whatever I want." Those nights, I pretended to still sleep as we drove home because I didn't want the tension between my parents to spark into a new war. I thought perhaps moving to the new house would make my parents happier and provide more space between them, but I realized that something between them never worked, which opened up their relationship to fidelity and eventual sickness.

When I thought nothing could stop my parents' constant fighting, I thought wrong. When Daddy learned that Mama was sick, he grew more docile and patient. I assumed that he felt bad fighting with his wife when she didn't have the energy or health to do it back. Other than the fact that they fought less each week, she began to eat the white starch she used for ironing and started smoking cigarettes. She knew that it hurt her lungs, but she didn't care about harming her body anymore. Mama must've believed eating the starch helped her in some way, but she never explained herself. Most of us didn't know that she was sick because she kept it hidden so well. We didn't notice her increase in visits to the bathroom or her more frequent cramps and gas. For the time being, none of us complained about the peace and quiet in the house.

I was 11 years old when I noticed the bloodstains on Mama's clothing. She had started bleeding from her rectum and couldn't hide it from us. While she often played it off and told us not to worry, we all watched over her to make sure that she didn't get any worse. Mama grew weaker as the days went on and had to sit down more when moving about the house. She also felt more lethargic and often wanted to rest rather than clean or cook. We knew her situation had gotten worse when she asked Darlene and Linda to take over running the household for her. Darlene had married and moved away already while Linda was in school at the time. Mama asked Darlene to raise Shannon, our youngest brother, alongside her son because they had only a year between them. Knowing Daddy couldn't handle raising five children on his own and feeling the pressure from Mama to step up, she ended up raising Shannon, Patricia, and Jamie. Linda, on the other hand, dropped her education and took over all household responsibilities. Not long after this change, Mama's sickness took a toll on her body, and we had to hospitalize her. Perhaps she wanted to make sure we would survive without her before giving into her need for treatment.

Before long, Mama found herself living out of her hospital room, and Daddy and I tried to visit her as often as we could to normalize her experience. My other siblings, except Linda, didn't go to visit Mama as much because they had their own business to handle. After school on one of those days, my cousin and I got off the bus and waited out in the yard for Daddy to get home. Various smells wafted out of the kitchen and into the yard and made our stomachs growl. We knew that Linda would have something delicious waiting for us when we returned from the hospital. Daddy pulled into the driveway about an hour later, and my cousin and I hopped into the backseat together. He backed up once more and drove towards Spartanburg General. Inside the car, a country station played on the radio, and Daddy had one hand on the wheel as he glanced out the window at the people passing by. I hoped that Mama couldn't sense when her husband's eyes wandered because she would explode on us upon our arrival to her hospital room. The last time we visited, they had connected machines and dripping tubes to her arms. Sh couldn't get out of her hospital bed for much, except to hurry to the bathroom a few feet away. I had hoped that she would fight her sickness and return home to us soon.

When we arrived that day, I saw no change in her condition. She looked tired and almost sunken in, as if her body withered away. My cousin and I both gave her gentle hugs, not wanting to hurt her in any way.

I said, "Hi, Mama."

"Hey, baby. It's so good to see you."

The room had a particular smell about it, mixed in with her musty scent, but I swear it smelled like rot. Linda explained to me later that the smell came from Mama herself. At that age, I had a limited attention span, and I didn't like seeing Mama in her weak state. Often, my cousin and I would play around in the room while Daddy talked with her. Since she moved into the hospital, Daddy has grown cautious in order to not set her off so often and make her situation worse. I should've given her more of my time and acted with more maturity during our visits because while she appreciated my continual presence, I didn't show her the proper love and respect she deserved. By the time that I realized it, she had already gone into coma, and soon after, she passed away. She was only 42.

Linda had seen Mama last before she passed away. According to her, Mama had begged my sister to leave her on the day she died. After getting tired of her persistence, Linda gave in and left the hospital. She swore that Mama sent her away so that she wouldn't watch her die. Wanting to check in again, Linda went back to the hospital later that day and found out that our Mama had passed. Once my sister accepted her loss, the nurses told her that right before Mama died, she rose out of her coma and spoke.

"Mama, are you coming to take me home?" she asked as if talking to a spirit.

According to the staff, she then fell back down on the bed, unmoving, and transitioned onto the afterlife, led by the woman who raised her and taught her how to be a good mother. They suspected that she had colon cancer. Upon getting the news, the whole house fell into a solemn silence filled with sobbing, staring in shock, and feeling her absence.

Soon after her death and the funeral, neighbors came by to show their support and give their respects. The $200 checks started arriving in the mail, based on Mama's will. She wanted to make sure that her children could survive without her. We didn't know what to do with our sudden influx of money, and Daddy tried to take those checks away and spend them how he saw fit. To my dismay, it didn't take long for him to start spending time with new women. Granted, I believe he stayed faithful during Mama's sickness, all the way up until the moment we put her in the ground. We didn't like how he had moved on with such ease, but no one confronted him about it until he tried to take our money and spend it on the women he dated. Linda stood up to him, as the most responsible woman of the house, and fought him. She knew that the oil heater that kept the house warm needed oil, so she spent the checks for that reason. That being said, Daddy sometimes succeeded in taking our checks and left us to freeze in the cold house. In many ways, our family went downhill without Mama's stabilizing presence. All my siblings scattered to the wind and moved on in whatever ways they could. Only Daddy and I remained in Mama's house, and for as long as we kept it, I made sure to preserve her memory, no matter how hard Daddy tried to forget it.

Inside Peach Bowl Lanes

When I look back at my youth, sometimes I think about how Mama would've reacted had she found out about the mischief I got into during those years. I imagine that from Heaven, she looked down upon me with a mixture of rage and disappointment, itching to whip me with her heavenly extension cord. Her ever-present gaze from above always made the guilt I felt that much worse. At the time, I had no steady parental guidance to keep me on the right track. After Mama's death, Daddy filled his loneliness by picking up an array of women at various clubs and disappearing with them on the weekends. He didn't care to support me in any way, so I survived because of the checks I received from Darlene each month. Thus, at the age of 14, I learned how to take care of myself without the help of adults. That, however, didn't mean that I knew the best ways to live. I had the house all to myself most of the time, though Daddy would come and go from work during the weeks. On Fridays, he would come home with his fresh paycheck, grab a loaf of bread and an egg, and leave me alone the rest of the weekend. He always came back on Sunday nights broke with no food or oil to warm the house. The first few times, I tried to stop him from leaving by grabbing hold of him and begging him to care for me, but he would just shove me away and leave me standing alone in the driveway as he pulled away in his car. I never knew where he went until he brought the first woman back home with him. Like the perfect roommate, I stayed out of their way and ignored the noises that emanated from his room down the hallway. When the women would slink out of his room in the mornings, I always made sure to hide outside to avoid bumping into them. When Daddy went to work each day, I didn't always attend school because he didn't care about my health or education. On top of that, he never bought food for me, so I had to make do on my own. Not knowing how to cook, I often bought canned foods and snacks to keep myself fed. At this time, I didn't have my priorities straight because I cared more about spending my money on pool and pinball rather than quality food for myself. Some- times, I would spend almost all my monthly check on games before I would remember that I needed to buy my food for the month. This shortage of funds led to many days spent with an empty stomach. Overtime, I thinned out and returned to weighing 100 pounds.

Uncle Jim must've sensed my desperation at that time because without my asking, he started showing up at the house and would take me to his girlfriend's place for food. I liked to imagine that Mama sent him a message from Heaven that told him to take care of me. Every day after school, I would wait outside on my front porch for him to pull up, and the minute I saw his car, my heart would jump with relief.

At my Uncle's and his girlfriend's dinner table, I learned a lot about them. For one, I didn't know that my Uncle served in the U.S. Army. However, when I asked him to tell me about it, his girlfriend always interrupted and changed to subject, in order to stop her boyfriend from beginning one of his rants. I learned from her that many people saw Uncle Jim as crazy because he thought that the government listened in on its citizens via their electronics. He apparently brought some of the war home with him. Uncle Jim didn't trust anyone, including his girlfriend, until years later when he married her. Each meal we shared together, he would switch plates with me without telling me that he feared his girlfriend had poisoned his food.

He would say, "Just in case."

I never understood why he thought she had it out for him because I grew to like his girlfriend. She worked at Duncan Elementary and often brought food home from the cafeteria for me to eat. At one point, Uncle Jim confronted Daddy about not performing his parental duty in taking care of me. I never asked my uncle if he'd let me stay with him rather than him taking me back to the cold house every day. He lived in a tiny, brick house and didn't have enough room for me. Even more so, I recognized that he had done a lot for me so far, so I didn't want to push my luck with his generosity.

As time went on, I stopped attending school at all and instead spent most of my time at the nearby bowling alley. I had constant entertainment, and my cousins Tony, Jay, and Tyrone all worked there. Mr. Cobb, the manager, took a liking to me right away and often allowed us to play free games of pool and pinball. He would gather all us kids around, take quarters out of the machines, and would throw them onto the floor to watch us scramble for them like pigeons. He even kept the bowling alley open after hours for us to use, which made him quite the popular manager. However, as I spent more time with my cousins, they told me about Mr. Locke's dark secret: He skims from the bowling alley's profits. Looking back on it now, I can see that his kindness went a long way to buy our silence. Samuel, the owner of the business, came around the bowing alley sometimes and would watch us play pool on occasion. He would bet $20 on me to win and never asked for money back if I lost. When he heard that Mama had passed away, he offered me a job. I needed the income to keep myself fed and to sustain my gaming habit, so I took the opportunity without hesitation. My responsibilities began with sweeping and mopping the floors, fixing the lanes when pins and bowling balls got jammed, and after some time, cleaning and fixing the machines. I proved myself as a hard worker and must've impressed Samuel because one day, he told me that he wanted to adopt me. I didn't see his offer coming, and neither did Daddy nor my sisters. Despite being offered a chance to live a better life, I never voiced my opinion about Mr. Samuel's proposal. In the end, my non-existent guardians declined his offer, despite my minor disappointment.

As I thought my life would fall back into its same routine, one of my brothers reentered my life in a major way. Jamie, more because of consequences rather than by choice, returned to our home and started living with me again. Darlene started sending him his checks, but we kept our money separate rather than combining our funds to purchase certain necessities for the house, like oil, which we didn't know how to buy. Because I knew Daddy would steal his food if he left it out, I made sure that Jamie hid his junk food under his mattress. At night, the house had no electricity or heat, so my brother and I would huddle together in the same bed and use the living room rug to stay warm, despite its filthiness. When he learned that I go to work rather than school, my brother decided to take the same route, having no interest in pursuing his education. He started coming to the bowling alley with me and obtained a job there in no time. Even more important to me at the time, Jamie became a pool master. In the end, my brother managed to pull me out of the pit of loneliness I had found myself in since Mama's death. He didn't, however, stop me from making some bad decisions that came soon after our reunion.

I blame my cousins and their effective peer pressuring for getting me into trouble. Taking inspiration from Mr. Locke's ability to steal from the bowling alley under Samuel's nose, my cousins and I began taking money from the cash box behind the counter. We took

$40-$50 many times without anyone's noticing, so I didn't think anything of it when we tried again. According to my cousins, it was my turn to steal from the box, and they promised to keep watch for Mr. Locke or Samuel from their spot beside the main booth. I lowered onto my hands and knees, crawled like an infant on the patterned, carpet floor, and made my way under the adjustable counter. The bowling alley had customers, but no one seemed to pay us any mind. Mr. Locke operated the cash register and managed the shoe rentals but not at that moment. We knew that throughout the day Mr. Locke would move the cash from the register to the tin box beneath the counter for Samuel to collect at the end of each day. I shimmied over to the box and found it unlocked as usual. Upon opening it, I took our usual amount from the stack and then closed the box so that nothing looked amiss. I should've folded the cash up and hid it in my back pocket until we could split it up. Instead, I maneuvered my way out, thinking nothing had gone wrong because my cousins stood watch, and bumped right into Samuel as he glared at me. Knowing he caught me red handed, I handed him the money but couldn't find the words to explain. Mr. Locke materialized out of nowhere and came to my defense right away. When I glanced back at my cousins, they all looked at me as if I had done something wrong.

As Mr. Locke continued to explain the situation, Samuel stated, "I'm calling the police."

Samuel stormed off with Mr. Locke on his heal. I could hear Mr. Locke saying, "Please, sir. There's no need to involve the cops. We can handle this matter in house."

With the adults gone for the moment, my cousins came over to me and threatened to beat me up if I exposed their involvement. Their father would've beaten them if he'd found out about their crimes. In addition, Mr. Locke knew that I could expose his theft to the police or Samuel so he did his best to keep me from an arrest. He succeeded in the end, but they fired me to no surprise. I stopped hanging around there because I couldn't handle the thought of facing Samuel, my once potential adoptive father, or my guilt. Jamie managed to keep his job at the bowling alley, so I decided to go to school again and spend time with other people.

Turns out, reconnecting with people from your past can offer some reprieve. I ended up reconnecting with Robbie and his brother Emmitt. They both had light skin and huge hair, and they acted like such players when they would drive to school in their grandfather's 1970s Oldsmobile. Of course, neither had their driver's license during this time, but that didn't stop them from rolling down the windows and blaring their favorite songs from the Isley Brothers, Rick James, and Earth, Wind, and Fire. They often skipped school like I did, but they would sometimes give me lifts to the new pool hall that opened up down the road. Where they went beyond that, I didn't keep track. They tried to impress girls back then, and I'd often hear stories about the women they had been with when I'd visit their home. I had no such experience, and my friends knew that. However, I liked hanging with them because their grandpa kept the house warm. We adopted it as our frequent hangout spot.

That all changed, however, when Robbie got a girl named Bethany pregnant. I didn't recognize her as someone from our school, but I knew Robbie and Emmitt liked messing around, so I should've seen it coming. Soon after he learned the news, my friend quit school and started working at the meat packing company his brother and father worked at, in an effort to provide for his future child and its mother. That being said, working a day job didn't stop Robbie from wandering and maintaining his prior habits with women. Bethany learned of his trespasses soon enough when one of the women confronted her. It planted a seed of revenge in her mind that came to fruition after she had given birth to her son.

In the year I turned 18, I had one year of school left, managed to get my driver's license thanks to my cousin Tony letting me borrow his Oldsmobile Cutlass, and spent my last check and some savings, around $300, to purchase a Pinto from Darlene. During this important time of my life, I also experienced sex for the first time.

Bethany had always low-key flirted with me when we spent time together as a group. When she showed up on my doorstep one day, out of the blue, I didn't know what to say. I always admired her long, dark hair, her curved body, and her flirty, aggressive personality, but I never voiced my thoughts to her. Robbie remained unfaithful to her, which led her to knock on my door that day.

"Hey, Heyward. How's it going?" she asked.

She made it obvious what she wanted, and one thing led to another. Afterwards, we agreed to let nobody know, and for her, she could feel like she got back at her son's father. She taught me how to kiss, how to make love, and how to enjoy a relationship with a woman. I feared that Robbie would find out because I knew he'd punch me for it, and I would lose his friendship. We had one narrow escape with Tony, but he kept my secret in loyalty to me as a relative. However, the sex felt amazing, and I liked it too much to stop. It felt like a game. I started driving my Pinto to her mother's house down the street up until I wrecked it after one too many drinks, and the other half of the time, she walked over to my cold house to visit. Despite his cheating, Robbie ended up moving in with Bethany and her mom in order to help raise his son. She spent the days with me and spent the nights with him, and she grew more conflicted every day we met.

Despite the distraction of entertaining my secret girlfriend, I earned my high school diploma and obtained a summer job with Meals on Wheels. I started to cook and clean dishes for three dollars an hour, which in the end helped me because I learned how to make food for myself through working there. Although, I hated washing the dishes because we had to use scolding, hot water and disinfecting soap cubes to get rid of germs and make sure tuberculosis wouldn't spread more. I didn't work there long, however, and I gave up my position to my big sister Lena. I had a quick stint at a furniture store that lasted six months. My next job came from my friend Ben, after I helped him clean out some warehouses. He told me that he had several companies that needed their offices cleaned each week, so he brought me onboard to assist him. Right when I felt that I found stability in my life, Daddy gave me the news that we couldn't keep Mama's house any longer. Daddy and Darlene hadn't made payments on it for a long time, and the owner Mr. Bleu planned to evict us. I went to speak with him soon after I found out and tried to convince him that I could make the payments on the house now that I had two jobs. Mama and him knew each other from school and co-bought our house when we moved in. However, he didn't seem convinced.

He said to me, "Heyward, you're a brave man for coming up here and trying to make this work. If you were making a little bit more money, I would give the house to you. "

Instead, Mr. Bleu sold the house to my sister Doris, who ended up fixing it up, adding onto it, and then selling it as soon as she could. It hurt me deep down to see Mama's house go to someone else. It pained me even more to move out. After abandoning the house that Mama loved, Daddy, Jamie, and I moved into a local trailer park. Daddy went back to his typical, philandering routine, and Jamie stopped working at the bowling alley and instead found work at a mall. Bethany didn't mind my new residence and continued to come visit me at the trailer. In order to avoid suspicion, she would park in the Bilo parking lot rather than in front of our place. She still felt conflicted about whether she should stay with her son's father, despite his cheating, or whether she should move in with me, her lover.

Her dilemma remained until the day she came over and said, "Heyward, I'm going to have to quit seeing you."

I replied, "If you're going to quit seeing me, can we have sex one last time?"

That one last time led to the birth of my first son, Jonathan, and because I never revealed my relationship to Bethany to anyone, my son grew up with Robbie as his father. Even to this day, I haven't had the courage to tell Robbie the truth, and it ended up causing Jonathan and my other children a lot of pain and hurt.

Upon stepping into adulthood, I often looked back at the year I spent with Bethany and felt a mixture of longing and shame. When I thought about Mama, I could imagine the disappointment she would feel towards our losing her house.

Beside the Battery Plant

Sometimes, opportunities with clear potential hide a fouler truth that lingers underneath. For some time, I still worked with Ben and cleaned the offices of various companies. For two years, I would take out the trash, sweep and mop the floors, clean the bath- rooms, and then proceed to another office. I found the work tedious and unpleasant, but it paid the bills. One time, when I went to clean the offices of the Greer power company, the manager John came out of his office, noticed my good work ethic as I cleaned, and offered me a full-time position with their company. Seeing the chance to earn a better income for myself and work longer hours, I accepted in a heartbeat, but at that age, I didn't think to consider the repercussions. I often cleaned the offices in the evenings after they had closed, so I never had to interact with any of the employees. Even when I did, I often moved around without drawing their attention. Anyone entering a new work environment for the first time won't know what to expect beforehand, but I never could've anticipated the subtle animosity my fellow coworkers would show me down the line. Any moment I went beyond what they considered racially acceptable, the distaste they had hidden from me before came out into the open.

John started me on the Tree Crew with a man named Steve, and at first, everything seemed kosher. He had me running brush and picking up the debris that fell. This kept branches and trees from falling on our power lines and lowered the chances of power outages in the future. Lifting up logs like this for so many years ended up hurting my back overtime. After five years of backbreaking work, Jeff moved me onto a service truck with two men named Marty and Zachary. Marty trained me when I first started, but I didn't feel like I had learned much from him. I could tell that he didn't want to teach me at all. Overtime, I learned the art of trade by reading instruction manuals and watching my coworkers operate, along with some trial and error. If we had a problem to solve, then I would work until I solved it. They often alternated me to the Bucket Crew, which meant they had me repairing streetlights and fixing power lines that connected to homes. As I gained more experience, I learned how to set up poles between power lines and hang capacities. Working with Marty and Zachary, I learned that Marty liked to handle the "trouble calls," which most often meant that a customer had lost their power. Zachary preferred the Tree Crew, due to its lack of electrical work and lesser danger. Anytime we had to handle power lines that had fallen or blown out, neither of them wanted to take the risk, so I ended up doing most of the hazardous work myself. I feared electrocution, but I needed to do my work well in order to keep the job that I had learned to love.

When we found ourselves at the office, my coworkers and I would sometimes go out front in the parking lot during our lunch breaks and either shoot baskets or play football. If any of them had a problem with my skin color then, they didn't voice it or do anything about it. At the time, the power company had seven other African American employees on the staff, but none of them worked on either of the crews as I had. I defied the odds of my race, and I felt pride towards my position.

Often, they would tell me, "Well done, Heyward" or "You're doing good work, Pearson. Keep it up."

The job came with its risks, but the pay made it worth it. Out of all the tools and equipment I used on the job, my gloves saved my life the most. I carried multiple sets at a time, but the ones I used most often had a pinhole in them that would absorb the electricity from the wires. I remember how the electricity felt as it traveled through the gloves. It took a lot of willpower to remain calm any time it happened. Rain always made working on lines worse, due to our gloves getting slippery and the rain obscuring our vision. However, most of our work occurred because of storms, and at the power company, we worked to satisfy our customers.

At the end of each workday, I would go home to the trailer that I shared with Daddy and Jamie. They both had jobs like I did, so for most of the day, our home sat empty. With the three of us living there, we could afford it, but it came with drawbacks. First off, fitting three grown men into one trailer got crowded sometimes. Despite that, Jamie and I had the place to ourselves most weekends and some evenings because Daddy would do his disappearing act and spend nights elsewhere. Worst of all, the trailer park we lived in sat next to the Battery Plant. It always released smoke into the air and left a haze over the area. It also created an acidic smell that would burn our throats and noses and give us headaches. We had a sewer manhole right next to our trailer, which the county never sent anyone to close. Because we didn't have an air conditioner, we had to sleep with our windows open during warm nights. When I reported the smell to the DHEC, the representative claimed that they never received a call from us. Thus, the chemicals continued to contaminate the air, water, and ground. We didn't have the income to move at that time, so we got used to it, despite the potential detriment to our health. If you breathe in a foul scent long enough, you don't notice it anymore.

Jamie worked at the local mall still, and one day, he brought a white girl home with him. She introduced herself as Janice, and I learned that her mom had kicked her out of the house and she needed a place to stay. We agreed to let her live in our trailer until she could get her feet underneath herself again. The days turned to weeks and into months, and Janice and I grew to know each other well. I didn't have the heart to throw her out on the street again. I also didn't mind having a pretty woman around, and she seemed interested in me.

When I asked her why she stayed, she answered, "You're mine, and I'm not leaving you."

I found her boldness arousing, and it spurred our casual friendship into something more, so much so, that my sisters found out. All my sisters, except Darlene, expressed concern towards my interest in Janice. For starters, they thought that my dating outside my race would cause trouble. At this point, Patricia also suspected that I had fathered Jonathan, and because of this, she wanted me to get back with Bethany to help raise him. I dismissed her assumption because even if it held an ounce of truth, it would upend all of our lives. I remained with Janice in the end, despite knowing that our relationship may cause problems at work. By the time that Janice and I needed some privacy, I had worked at the power company for two years and earned enough money to rent a separate trailer each month. It felt like a step in the right direction because now I could establish my own family with Janice by my side. In my mind, no one at work needed to know. A single phone call changed everything. One day, I left our trailer to head to work, but I noticed that my Cutlass Oldsmobile had a flat tire. I cursed my poor luck and got the spare out of the trunk to change it. I knew doing so would make me late for work, but I had no other choice. Considering how I had never shown up to work late before, I doubted anyone would have a problem with it. As I used the jack to lift the car and removed the tire's lugs with the wrench, I heard the landline ring a few times inside before Janice picked it up and answered.

I didn't think anything of it until she opened our front door and called, "Heyward, Mariahlynn is on the phone. She's wondering when you'll be coming in."

Mariahlynn was John's secretary at the office, and she had never called before. I answered her back, "Tell her I'm almost done changing my tire and will be there in 20."

Janice disappeared inside, and I hurried to finish replacing the tire on my car so that I could book it to work. By the time I arrived, I noticed a change in the atmosphere the moment I entered the room with my fellow coworkers. They all stared at me like I had committed a crime and would pummel me at any second. It didn't take long for me to learn that Mariahlynn had assumed the color of Janice's skin by talking with her on the phone and spread rumors to the entire office about my dating a white woman. I tried to ignore the matter at first, but I couldn't avoid it for long because John ordered me into his office.

With clear disdain in his face and posture, he asked, "Heyward, what do you have in your pockets?"

"Nothing, sir," I replied in confusion.

John stepped up close to me and rummaged through each of the pockets on my jacket and pants. I didn't want to lose my job so I allowed him to do so.

When his search came out fruitless, he stated, "If you have a white woman up there, I will fire you on the spot."

Without confirming anything to him, I nodded and left his office in haste. The rest of my workday went on as usual, but both Marty and Zachary talked to me less and looked at me with disdain. From that day onward, their prejudice towards me got worse, and my white coworkers did everything in their power to try to get me fired. For one, Mariahlynn loved to taunt me when others couldn't see it. She would lift her skirts and show me her white legs in a provocative way. I knew that no one would believe me if I wrote her up for sexual harassment, so I told the other African Americans on staff about it. They thought that she wanted to sleep with me, but I couldn't see it as anything more than her trying to get me into trouble. On top of her visual assaults, John's daughters sometimes came to the office after hours to see me for some odd reason. I never showed them any attention, despite their constant flirting, but that didn't stop the other men from making crude jokes about it. They made it sound like I wanted to take the girls home with me. To my knowledge, John never heard about their lies nor did he learn about his daughters' behavior towards me. However, in the back of my mind, I wondered if John had used them as bait in order to have a reason to fire me, but I had no proof of that. The girls stopped coming around after they realized I had no interest in them, which gave me a temporary breath of fresh air.

The men in my office acted with no more maturity than the women. Whereas the women came at me with their looks, my male coworkers came for my honor. Anytime we found ourselves at the office, Brett, one of John's sons, would take his wallet out of his pant's pocket and set it on the top of his desk's truck bins. He never did this before the rumors. He would leave it sitting there and try to catch me looking at it in the wrong way. His bait didn't ever work, however, but that didn't stop him from trying. Anytime anything went missing, they always blamed me first.

One day, I went out to hang a streetlight with Zachary and my coworker Carl, who had replaced Marty on our service truck. We took the job around noon, so after the work, we all went our separate ways to get lunch. Carl returned to the office early and decided to clean the service truck. Not wanting to get our equipment wet, he set our toolbox on the back of another truck, but no one saw him do it. When that truck drove away and the tools went missing, no one could find it. We knew that we had them before lunch, so Carl accused me of taking them. TJ, the manager who took over after John, threatened to fire me for taking it, despite the fact that I denied the accusation. Before anything happened, the contractor who owned the truck showed up, gave the toolbox back to TJ, and explained how they found it on the rear of their truck. TJ and Carl never apologized for blaming me, and on top of that, they made me paint the inside of the substation because he had nowhere else to put me, due to the prejudice. I should've felt relieved that he didn't fire me instead, but I couldn't get over the fact that they still punished me after I did nothing wrong. I knew that they saw this hiccup as a chance to punish me for my alleged relationship with a white woman. I stayed there for six months. When I grew fought up with the disrespect, I brought the issue to Jeff, our new CEO, in hopes to gain his trust and tell him the truth straight- away. He understood my plight, but he didn't think talking to my coworkers would make my situation any better, so I dropped it.

When I would go home each day to Janice, I couldn't help but complain about the injustices done to me. She would comfort me the best she could, but she couldn't stop them from bullying me without leaving me altogether. Her presence in my life brought along an intense level of prejudice that I hadn't experienced at any of my other work places in the past. Because of her unemployment and skin color, she didn't have to experience the pressure.

I had told Jeff about my relationship with Janice, but I didn't want my other coworkers to see Janice and I together out in public because it would bring me nothing but trouble. Anytime she had to go into town, I didn't go with her in fear of someone seeing us. Just the thought of someone catching me stressed me out all hours of the day. Janice asked to go out often, but we ended up staying in most of the time. On occasion, we would travel to Greenville because I felt safer appearing in public there. My paranoia did put a strain on our relationship, and it only got resolved with the help of our first-born child. When Janice found out about her pregnancy, it came as a surprise to both of us. We had not married yet, and neither of us felt prepared to raise a child. However, I felt stable enough in my job situation that I knew I could provide for both of them. The moment Kayla came into the world, I promised myself that I would love her with all my heart. Janice and I also agreed to make it work so that we could give our daughter the life she deserved. Before we knew it, we had two more children in the next four years: our boy Juwan in 1993 and our youngest Kimberly in 1994. While Janice carried Juwan, we got married to ensure the stability of our family.

Sometimes, I think back to their childhoods and smile. During the summer weekends when we had good weather, we would spend time outside together and have cookouts. I would get the grill out and the kids would play in the kiddie pool. Janice would splash the children with the hose and make them laugh with glee.

Kayla would yell, "More, Mommy! More!"

Then, they'd dry off by playing basketball while still wearing their bathing suits. One time, we took a day trip to Myrtle Beach. I remember hanging out on the beach all day and chasing the kids about in the sand. They didn't want to stay still, just like the little sand crabs scurrying over the dunes.

My coworkers at the power company didn't appreciate my chil-dren as much as I did. When we had Kayla, Marty found out somehow and made sure everyone knew that I had a baby by a white woman. My torment renewed, but they didn't come at me with any new threats. However, they did assign me to work construction with Brett, a man who I knew didn't like me. He reported to TJ, who I also didn't have a good history with, but my boss had Brett update him on my work ethic from time to time. I've always believed that I stayed a "C line- man" rather than a "B" because of him. As wrong as it felt to gratify this man, I needed to get on his good side somehow. I ended up purchasing an air conditioner unit from him, but when he arrived at my trailer to drop it off, he wouldn't help me install it. I even bought a car from him without a booster in it. No matter how hard I tried to win him over, he never saw past my marriage to a white woman. One day on the job, I burnt a pair of Brett's pliers on accident. I bought him a new pair, but he reported it anyway and made it sound like I did it on purpose. Luck took my side that day, however, because my replacing the pliers kept me out of trouble. While I won that battle, Brett continued to make fun of me. In the summer, he would make racist remarks about my wearing white sunscreen, and when I wore glasses instead and got tan, he called me Spot. One of my other co- workers kicked me from behind one day, but I couldn't do anything to him in return.

Their constant suspicions about me stealing put me on edge all the time, so much so that my paranoia about going to public places remained. Twice my children injured themselves in terrifying ways and had to go to the hospital, and yet, I couldn't bring myself to go with Janice either time. I didn't go to the grocery store or to doctor appointments. On top of that, we started to fight more often. She would beg me to go out more, and I would beg her to get a job, but neither of us did. I feared someone would see us together and then electrocute me on the job. Even more so, I needed to keep that from happening so I could support us, unlike her. I found her peer pressure and lack of financial support crippling, and Janice couldn't take it anymore and moved out. With her absence, I had to manage working a full-time job while also providing for my children as a single father. It pushed me to my limits as a provider, but I didn't let that obstacle stop me from moving forward, for the sake of my children.

Onto 203 Gemini Way

My kids didn't understand why their mother had left them and understandably grew angry towards her absence, but I reminded them that she still loved them very much. I also guaranteed them that our separation had nothing to do with them. Because Janice didn't have a job and the kids ended up in my custody, I had to explain this truth to them. On the work front, the prejudice I experienced at work decreased as my coworkers' loathing for me turned to pity, as they knew that I had to take care of three children on my own. As their badgering lessened, I didn't feel like complaining about it any- more because my children couldn't understand. I stopped drinking all together and lost a lot of weight, but I still smoked on occasion. I had my kids stay in the after school program each day, which would give me enough time to pick them up after work, and Daddy would take care of the kids if I ever had to go out. Sometimes, I would get calls from school and have to take time off to take care of my children when they needed medical attention. Thankfully, the power company had a "Families in Crisis" program that helped me pay for the bills. At one point, I did try to get Janice to pay child support, but because she never did and would've ended up in jail because of it, I dropped the case altogether. I allowed her to still have visitations with the kids when she decided to show up, which allowed her to form better relationships with them later on in life. Instead of lingering on the past, I looked towards the future and took steps to improve my family's quality of life.

The first step was getting my family out of the contaminated trailer park. In the nine years I spent living there, I found love and raised my three, beautiful children between its vinyl walls. That being said, I couldn't wait to leave. We spent three more years in the trailer after Janice left before I had enough money saved to move. Had Daddy been willing to move in with me and help me save up money rather than spend all of his time chasing women, we could've moved sooner. However, not long after we argued about it, his situation changed significantly. He had been driving without insurance one day when a woman hit his vehicle. Nothing bad came of the situation then, but he grew worried that the police would catch him for driving without insurance and throw him in jail. He worked as janitor at the time, and while at work, he ended up having a stroke. They took Daddy to the hospital and gave me a call to inform me of his situation.

"Mr. Pearson, your father's had an accident."

No one ever likes hearing those words over the phone. I didn't know it at the time, but his decline in health would affect my life thoroughly over the next decade. Once they discharged him from the hospital, he moved in with Linda for a time, as he was unfit to live alone in his trailer any longer. He didn't last two months in her household because neither of them got along, and she didn't like how he would spit on the walls and floor. Eventually, she told him to leave, and by the time he had lost his job and started having mini strokes, he finally agreed to move in with me. His new situation wasn't ideal for me, but he had no one else to take care of him. By 2000, I purchased the house at 203 Gemini Way for our family to live in. We gave it to the kids as a Christmas surprise, and they looked forward to living someplace bigger where they wouldn't have to share beds or smell acidic fumes in the air. In my eyes, the house had everything we needed: one story, three bedrooms, two bathrooms, a two-car garage, a hilly backyard, a porch, and a community. No one at work believed that I could afford the house and claimed that I stole money from the company. Their allegations had no proof, so I didn't let their jealousy ruin my good situation. On top of that, I believed that Mama would've loved seeing us in a nice house again, and it made everything that much better.

Unfortunately, my hectic daily schedule didn't improve with the new house, and my routine became a burden. Like before, every morning began at 5 and started with getting my children dressed for school. None of my kids liked waking up early, and it made them uncooperative. I would help each of them get dressed and make sure that they brushed their teeth well. Often, my nieces would braid my daughters' hair on the weekends, and their hair would stay like that for days. Otherwise, I would do my best and put their hair up in a three-way ponytail with two of the ponytails sticking out on the sides and one poking out in the back. Kayla would let me do her hair and pick out her clothes, but then she'd change them when she got to school. After everyone had clothes on and ate their cereal, I would go about getting ready for work. With that done, I would make sure Kayla got on the bus, drop Juwan and Kimberly off at elementary school, and arrive in the power company's parking lot by eight. After work, I would pick up my children from the after school program, where the staff would be give them a snack and supposedly helped them with their homework. That never happened of course because they had too many kids to watch. I tried to find them a better option but met only dead ends. From there, I would drive every- one home, handle any chores around the house, and help with any remaining homework. Due to my poor education as a boy, I always struggled with giving them any sort of help, but I tried my best to make sure that they did well in school. When Juwan wouldn't do his homework, I would whoop him as punishment. Moments like those always made me miss Janice. For dinner, I often alternated between cooking quick and easy meals like pot roast, bean casserole, sloppy joes, salads, and hamburger helper, or we would end up going out to eat. Only on Sundays would I fix bigger meals, which led to leftovers for the next week to come. Bathes followed dinner. Kayla and Juwan knew how to clean themselves, but I would bathe Kimberly until she got old enough to do it by her self. Every day ended with my kids brushing their hair and getting into their pajamas. Only then would I be able to take a breath, but it would already have struck ten.

By the time we moved into the new house, I didn't know what to do about Daddy's condition. He moved around fine and often took walks through the neighborhood. He didn't like that he couldn't drive or go anywhere by himself anymore, so he did his best to go outside the house when he could. Despite his exercising, however, he started having mini strokes. I'll never forget the first one I experienced; his mouth looked crooked, and he couldn't remember me. Because he had forgotten me, he hollered as if I wanted to mug him. I took him to the hospital that day and learned that it affected his memory and recall. As more of these mini strokes occurred, his memory grew worse, and they ended up paralyzing the entire right side of his body. When this happened, it felt like I had adopted a fourth child. I would have to help my father move around the house and take bathes, which I struggled with, due to his size and weight. Because he couldn't lift himself with his right arm or right leg, I would have to help him in and out of the bathtub. He always ended up taking a bath last because I'd have to clean the tub after he finished. In the mornings and nights, I also helped him dress because he couldn't move well enough to do it alone. I grew to resent Daddy, as I often remembered how he had abandoned me as a kid. I sometimes thought that he didn't deserve my kindness, but Mama had raised me to do the right thing. I remained by his side even if he didn't do the same for me in the past.

The family adjusted to our new lifestyle overtime. The girls and I got our own rooms, and Juwan and Daddy shared a room. My son often complained about sharing a bed with him because of his spitting, but he got over it after some time. My kids liked spending time with their grandpa while they still had him around because even they could see his health declining. While my kids went to school and stayed in the after school program, I had Daddy sent to an adult daycare. A woman came to pick him up every morning and took him to play bingo and cards with the other elderly staying there. They fed him and gave him something to do while I worked. I ended up giving the woman who drove him around a key because she always beat me home each day. From there, Daddy sat around and watched television. On the weekends, my kids played out outside on our lawn and hung out with the other kids in the neighborhood. Juwan rode his bike up and down our steep driveway, and I always warned him not to hit my new car. One day in particular, I had just finished washing it and had left it out to dry in the sun. He had a mountain bike that was double his size. He and Kayla stood outside together, and as he began to peddle down the driveway, Kayla slung one of my belts into one of his tires. Rather than flying out again, it wrapped around the tire and became tangled in the spokes. The front wheel locked up, stopped in place, and threw Juwan right over the handle- bars. The bike jerked to the side and came only inches from hitting my car. Neither of my kids told me about this incident in the moment, but if I had found out, it would not have been pretty for them. Sometimes, I watched them from the front stoop and remembered how they used to play hide and seek with other kids in that contaminated trailer park. In the new house, I didn't have to worry about any of that anymore. After everything, I managed to keep my family together, despite being a single father with an ever-disappearing income.

At work, people wondered how I could work a full-time job and keep up with my family at the same time. I never had an answer for them in the moment, but I know what I would've said to them. "It was desperation and perseverance."

In the back of my mind, I blamed my coworkers for ruining my first marriage. Had they not tormented me about my relationship with a white woman, I could've given her more of the social life she wanted. Anytime another white woman in the office showed interest in me after our separation, my coworkers would threaten my job. I also worried that they'd accuse me of stealing again and fire me because of it. My anger and fear, however, did not stop me from working as hard as I could. My boss moved me back and forth between construction work, underground work, and heavy construction, and I took the workload as best I could.

I also closed another chapter of my life shortly after moving into the new house. In 2003, Janice and I signed our divorce papers and cut ties legally. The meeting went well, and I still have a good relationship with Janice to this day. That being said, I looked forward to finding love again and finding much-needed support in my life. Around this time, I had taken Daddy to the hospital many times because of his mini strokes, and during one of these visits, they diagnosed him with Diabetes. With no help from my sisters, I realized that I couldn't take care of Daddy any longer, and I moved him into an Assisted Living facility about 30 miles away in Easley. Thankfully, his social security and retirement checks paid for it all, but he didn't like it because of the distance and no one except me would come and visit. He knew that he had pushed his siblings away by telling them that he didn't need their help, but despite his slighting me worst of all, I didn't plan to abandon him.

One time, he said to me, "I'd rather be dead because no one ever comes to see me, except you."

Yet, whenever I stood to leave after each visit, he would beg, "Please don't leave me."

To ease his loneliness, I would pick him up every other weekend so that he could stay with our family. I also tried to host family dinners with my sisters so that he could see them. His memory faltered often, but he never forgot to ask about his money and cars. It was these sort of selfish requests that continued to push my siblings further away. While I continued to support Daddy, I did intend to fill his space in my home with a more feminine presence.

My first attempt at dating came when I met Evette, a woman working at my kids' cafeteria. We met at church a while back, and she seemed to like me well enough. She gave my children free meals at school in order to help me out. However, I noticed that she looked through my beeper and called numbers back to see if I talked to other women. Everyone at church said that she had trust issues, and I didn't like her nosiness so I broke it off. Shortly after our breakup and her learning about my job, she stopped giving my kids free lunches, and I had to start paying. My second attempt at dating went better. My sister-in-law brought a friend named Lisa over one day and introduced us. I found her attractive, and I realized that we could help each other. Like me, she had been divorced before and was a single parent. Her son, Tim, had Cerebral Palsy, so she needed my help as well. Within four months of us dating, she moved out of her parents' house and in with my family and I. It worked out well for me because I ended up injuring my back after lifting some poles and wires up one day. All those years I spent on the Tree Crew running brush through the chipper finally caught up to me. I reported to my boss that I had back pain, and it took a month before they approved me seeing a doctor. After getting some testing and an MRI done, they approved my pin insertion and spinal fusion surgery. I had it completed in 2004, and because she once had the same operation before due to a car wreck and didn't have a job. Because of it, she had the knowledge and free time to help me. With her guiding hand, my recovery went well.

By the time I could've returned to work, my boss came over one day and offered to make me lead over a truck. This had never happened before, as he often gave the higher positions to my white coworkers over me. However, after spending 21 years working hard at the power company, I ended up retiring and going on disability instead. Doing so freed me up to spend more time with my family and Daddy. For one thing, Lisa and I ended up getting married after seeing each other for a year. Neither of us cared much for making it a spectacle, so we went to the courthouse and said our vows in front of a judge. She did, however, insist on getting a five-carat wedding ring for herself, so I ended up dropping $5,000 on buying one for her. Since leaving my job, I didn't worry as much about my coworkers seeing me around town with my wife. On occasion, our family would pack up the car and visit Myrtle Beach for a day trip. Trips like these showed me of how grown up Kayla had become over the years. Rather than playing in the ocean and sand like her siblings, she preferred to tan in the sun and stare at boys. I would try to not let her preening get to me. Additionally, I continued to visit Daddy multiple times a week. I ended up moving him from four different retirement homes until I could get him in one that sat closer to our home. That way, seeing him required less of a drive, and it made Daddy happier.

I lived in the house on Gemini Way for eight years before the thought of moving again ever crossed my mind. I had Lisa to thank for the idea. She and her mother had this dream of moving down to Atlanta together, and perhaps she felt that she could do anything because Obama just became the first African American president. I expressed my concern that my savings and retirement payments wouldn't cover a new house, and she guaranteed me that she would come into some money once she won a lawsuit she had filed. To persuade me further, she let me pick out the house. After searching online and making some calls, I ended up finding the perfect house in the suburbs of Gainesville, GA. I took a mortgage out to pay for it and waited to see the money Lisa promised she'd win. When we told the kids that we had plans to move to another state, they didn't like it. They didn't want to leave their friends behind and have to start fresh at new schools. However, because they lived under our roof, they didn't have much of a choice. Lisa had her mind set, so we picked up our lives and moved further south. I did whatever made the wife happy.

Through Gainesville, Tucker, Winnjay

Mistakes lead to perspective, but they also come with a bag of emotions that you have to contend with on a daily basis. I eventually found myself in this sort of situation, and yet, I could've avoided it if I had acknowledged the telltale signs in the moment. It began when we moved to Atlanta, and for a time, everything felt so new that I ignored the problems brewing underneath. Our $300,000 house had three stories and a basement, and every person in the family ended up with their own bedroom for the first time ever. Kayla, who had since moved in with her boyfriend, also had a room in case she ever came to visit. We had so much space, and everything shined with a fresh shade of paint and a glint of spotlessness. We lived on the outskirts of Atlanta in the city of Gainesville, so Lisa and the kids had many more options for food and entertainment. They could go to Lake Lanier right around the corner or take a drive down Highway 985 for a Braves game or for a fun night out on the town. They left the house often, but I didn't mind the peace and quiet. Because I didn't have a day job anymore, parenting grew much easier. My stress and worry levels decreased, and I got more sleep on a daily basis, which made me more patient during the daytime. It also left me available to take the kids to their schools and pick them up afterwards, cook meals alongside my wife, and listen to the kids' concerns. On occasion, Juwan and Kimberly would complain that they had no children to play with in the neighborhood nor did they like being the new kids at their middle school. I couldn't do anything to help them with making friends, but because I had time on my hands now that I had retired, I tried my best to give them a good time.

Once, I took them to Six Flags, the biggest amusement park in Georgia. I knew that all the walking around and the rides themselves would hurt my back, but I wanted my children to have fun. We didn't have anything like this back home so they couldn't hold in their excitement. I watched them disappear down the path for one ride and then come running back to me with their hair all over the place. Juwan and Kimberly could ride together so I often didn't have to get on the coasters. Instead, I would sit on the benches outside the rides, hold our bags and drinks, and wait for them to come back. The lines varied per ride, so I often tried to find some shade to sit under. The whole park sat on top of asphalt, so over the course of the day, it seeped the energy out of me. From shooting targets with water, spinning around on swings, to eating pretzels and nachos, my kids made sure they did everything. I couldn't tell you which ride they liked the best because they ended up riding them all. By the time we drove home, we all felt exhausted.

I'd also tried to get the kids out into nature and the area around which we lived. Gainesville neighbors Lake Lanier, the largest lake in Georgia, and I would often take the boys to fish. The city offers many different locations for people to fish and still maintain their privacy. We had a particular spot that we used where the water remained low at the bank so we could walk out over the rocks without worrying about falling. We brought some folding chairs and packed sandwiches so that we could spend the whole day there. If Juwan or Tim ever caught something, we'd celebrate and then release it rather than keep it to cook later. They never caught anything big enough to eat anyways. I hoped that by bringing the two boys together I could make them bond more because they often didn't get along at home. Juwan would boss Tim around and would force him to do his chores for him. In the end, the boys liked the competition of it, and I just liked spending time with them while I still could.

When Kayla approached Janice and I about her desire to move in with her boyfriend Anthony and stay in Spartanburg, I initially didn't like the idea. I had no problem with her boyfriend, but I couldn't believe that they wanted kids at such a young age. While she proposed her plan to us, I could only hear, "Dad, I'm grown up now. You need to trust me. I'm ready to start my own family."

Janice saw no problem with her idea and allowed Kayla to live with her in Spartanburg instead of moving her down to Atlanta with me. I didn't want to anger Janice nor push my daughter away so I agreed in the end. Whenever she came to visit or called to check in, she sounded happy with her relationship so that was good enough for me. Anytime I would think about my little girl having children, I also remembered how she used to splash around with joy in the plastic, inflatable pool we'd bring out in the summers. I couldn't believe how quickly time had passed or that my daughter had grown up into a beautiful, young woman.

It didn't take long for Lisa to take advantage of our new town and its opportunities. For one thing, she set herself up as a caretaker for the elderly. Because of the level of care she showed me during my recovery, I didn't find her choice in career surprising at all. I thought it fit her well, and I liked the fact that she would bring in money to help me pay off the mortgage, considering how she wanted to move here in the first place. I should've known better. First, the money that she guaranteed me she'd win in a lawsuit never came. I barely made end's meet on our mortgage payments each month. To make matters worse, I eventually realized that beyond the money I brought in, no payments came in from her supposed caretaker work. I considered the fact that she could've had a separate bank account, but based on her past reliance on me to pay for everything, I doubted that. Instead of providing for her family, she found herself in the company of other men. For the first six months since we moved to Georgia, she cheated on me without my knowing. The worst part: I only found out because she told me about it all — more like rubbed it in my face. I don't know what I did to her to deserve it, but it hurt me more than she probably knew. Even worse, her infidelity didn't end, and I couldn't stop her without upending the kids' lives, including her son. My patience lasted six months until the moment Lisa left town for an entire week without telling me where she was going.

When she came back, she explained, "I had a fantastic time in Myrtle Beach with the guy I told you about, and I've decided to move in with him."

My response sounded like, "What about the kids? What did I

ever do to you? You can't just leave us like this!"

Before I knew it, Lisa gathered up her son and disappeared with everything but the bedroom suit, including the car I helped her buy when we moved down here. I found myself out of the house when she moved everything, so when I returned to find the house empty, I didn't take it well. In my rage, I broke one of the house's windows. I covered it with a tarp for the time being and lied to the kids about how it happened. I contacted the bank and tried to get my money back for the house, but they couldn't help me. Disgusted by the expensive house that I had bought for Lisa, the kids and I packed up our remaining belongings and moved back home a month later. I abandoned the house, stopped making payments on it, and let it foreclose. I didn't think anything of it in the moment because of my anger, but I grew to regret it. By doing so, I ended up destroying my credit. Had I seen earlier that Lisa used me for the money, I would've saved myself from the well of regret and anger I felt during this time. The six years we spent together felt like a complete sham. In the end, the kids and I agreed that we didn't want anything to do with her, and we returned to what we found familiar.

I couldn't buy a new place to live because of my credit so my sisters stepped up and helped me out. We first moved in with Doris and her family who lived in Greenville. While I appreciated her kindness, I hated that my kids and I were homeless. I felt like I had failed them by falling in Lisa's trap, so I set my mind to getting them in their own house again as soon as possible, with the help of my monthly disability check. Juwan and Kimberly liked returning to South Carolina, but because Doris didn't live in Greer, they ended up in new schools once again. My son got a fresh start at a new high school, and he made it work. My son had plenty of confidence and swagger. His grades always came out as passing, so I never complained. He showed interest in playing sports, but he never asked me about them because he knew that we couldn't afford them. Nor could I transport him back in forth from practices and games because we only had one car at the time. Once again, I hated that I couldn't afford to give my kids every opportunity because Juwan could've shown a talent for basketball, but our situation didn't allow it. At home, between my family and Doris's, we had little space. No one ever had time alone, and we constantly fought over the television. Anytime I would consider renting a new place, I'd remember that my bad credit wouldn't allow it. I lost everything. I had moments where I would drown in the darkest parts of myself. Everything felt so hopeless to me, and in my worst moments, I wanted to end it all. However, I knew that Juwan and Kimberly needed me, so I strove to continue saving money, took steps to improve my credit ever so slowly, and suppressed the self-loathing simmering inside me.

After six months of living with Doris, my family and I saw a glimmer of hope in our future. While browsing online one day, I found out that the house at 113 Tucker Road had gone on the market. The house had one story and three bedrooms, which worked well for Juwan, Kimberly, and I. It also kept the kids in the same school district, which they wanted now that they both went to Hillcrest High School. I approached the woman who owned the place about renting the place, and she showed concern about my history with damaging the houses I've lived in. I ended up signing a contract that stated the owner had the right to report me to the police if I damaged anything, and only then did she agree to let us stay there.

Upon settling in, the kids appreciated having their own space again. I, however, didn't fare well. My mental state worsened over the course of the next year. I spent a considerable amount of time alone in the house, which allowed my thoughts to divert down turbulent paths. I would hear underlying voices reminding me of my past failures and how Lisa had manipulated me and ruined everything. I'd get so angry and upset, and they would tell me what to do. I grew so frustrated that I ended up knocking out all the windows of the house in order to silence the noise. It didn't stop, however, and I drove to Linda's house next. I tried to tell her about the voices in my head, but she wouldn't believe me. My temper exploded, and I smashed in the windows of my car. Worst of all, I threatened to kill her. Before I knew it, Linda had called the police and notified them of my location. The police saw me as a danger to others, so they threw the handcuffs on me, put me in the back of their squad car, and drove me to the Greenville County Detention Center. Juwan came to visit me at the jail soon after, and I gave him my credit card so that he and Kimberly could survive without me. The woman we rented from evicted us, so the kids packed up our belongings and moved in with Linda for the meantime. I knew that I had wronged our landlord, and while awaiting trial, I received a letter from her lawyer regarding paying for the damages. I wrote back and explained to them that I had a mental episode. In the end, they decided to drop their charge of malicious injury against me. Thus, when my trial came around, I only had to plead guilty for one count of assault and battery in the third-degree. I suspect that the judge saw the underlying, mental condition behind my behavior because he gave me a misdemeanor charge and a stint of two weeks in jail.

While inside, I tried to focus on the positive and ignore the whispers in the back of my mind. I still worried for my children in my absence, but I knew that I had raised them well enough to take care of themselves during this time. I realized that not all kids had a parent like me. Not long after my arrival, a young white boy came in, and he would refuse to bathe. He reeked of body sweat, and it stunk up the jail. He bunked with a black man who threatened to hurt him because of his smell and his long toenails. I felt bad for the kid, and I didn't want anyone to hurt him. In a way, I saw my son in this kid. He explained to me that taking a shower at the same time as the rest of us scared him. In response, I showed him how to use the shower and do so in a way that he can maintain his privacy. I made sure that he understood that none of the men would bother him if he took care of himself, and he listened to me like a little child. He ended up taking my advice because he blended in more from then on. Towards the end of my two weeks, I had gotten tired of eating sandwiches and boiled eggs. I wanted to see my kids again and give them hugs without having security guards watching me. Before my release, however, the judge from my trial requested that they bring me back for a second meeting. I walked into the courtroom with shackles attached to my arms and legs, and he ordered me to go to a mental health institution within three day's time after my discharge.

The county released me after I served my time, and I found my kids at Linda's house. I owed Juwan and Kimberly an explanation, but I could never find the words to tell them about it that would make sense to them.

If I had though, I would've said, "I never meant to hurt either of you. It's just the Devil has been speaking in my mind, and he makes me do bad things."

In the end, Linda agreed to let us live with her until I could get back on my feet. While I appreciated her generosity, she didn't provide us with the most pleasant living experience. The kids and I knew that we didn't have anywhere else to go, so we didn't complain and followed her house rules. Upon my release, my kids told me about how she didn't allow anyone to use the shower's hot water before she got home from work each day. I also knew that Linda's kids would come home sometimes and the house would grow overcrowded. Over the course of the two years we lived there, I tried to ease our way with her by paying for her groceries and bills. It felt good to contribute to something and be productive with the money I had earned.

I also knew that I needed help in order to guarantee my family's safety, so I didn't fight the judge's order. On the second day of my freedom, I looked up the nearest doctor's offices in the area, and I found that Greer Mental Health Facility sat closest to Linda's house. I didn't have to wait long before they evaluated me and ran their tests. I have that judge to thank because they diagnosed me with schizophrenia and clinical depression. Upon their recommendation, I checked into the local hospital so that they could find a proper medication for me to take. The doctor prescribed me many, but I refused to take them at first. I couldn't bring myself to believe that taking these pills would fix my problems. I couldn't stop the voices from controlling me, so I couldn't see how the medications would either. However, the doctor and the nurses attending to me convinced me that they would calm me down. I stayed in the hospital for two weeks while I adjusted to my medications, and my patience paid off. The voices in my head ceased, and I grew less suicidal. It helped with my nerves and calmed me down enough to regain control of myself. They informed me that drinking messed with my medicine, so I quit entirely. The doctor also explained that it would take some time before my body accepts the medications fully. I felt so relieved that the pills worked because in the past, my condition frightened my kids at night. They didn't understand why I lost control at times, but my diagnosis gave them an explanation they could comprehend. Linda still worried that I'd go crazy, due to my occasional mental episodes while regulating my medicine, but I didn't have any more slip-ups. By the time that I returned home, Kayla started coming around more often, and I always loved seeing her lovely face. I've continued to take my prescription for over 10 years to this day, and I will forever act as a champion for getting help.

My mental recovery led me to focus less on my health and more on the health of others. More specifically, I grew concerned about Daddy's well being. When we moved to Atlanta, we didn't visit him at all, but since moving back home, I tried to visit when I could and felt healthy enough to do so. Between my sisters and I visiting him over the course of the past three years, we all noticed that he seemed to catch continual colds and never look well. I wish that they had taken an interest in visiting him sooner so he didn't feel so lonely, but I never brought it up. We all just wanted to comfort him during his decline in health. By mid-2011, he ended up with pneumonia. The disease weakened his body, and we knew that he wouldn't live much longer. He experienced kidney failure shortly after getting sick and went into a coma. Over the course of the eight years he stayed in various elderly homes, I always resented him a little bit for not taking care of me as a kid. By the time he went into a coma, I felt like I should've said things to him that I never had the chance to.

"I was a better father than you ever were."

Perhaps it was for the best that I never told him that, but I hope that he realized it before his body began to shut down on him. He ended up passing away while Darlene sat by his side. I remember taking my kids to see him one last time as my sisters wept. We gave him a good, respectable funeral but didn't hesitate to move on with our lives.

I also closed the book on the most regrettable six years of my life. Lisa and I met for the first time since her disappearance and signed the divorce papers. I wanted nothing to do with her, and I left that meeting without saying anything else in order to avoid getting unpleasant with her. The last I heard, she ended up marrying the man she left me for. I figured that he would just be another man that she'll suck the savings out of, but that wasn't my problem.

At this point, I wanted to get back on my feet as my father's passing and my divorce freed me from the last two threads keeping me stuck in the past. I didn't want to feel that nothing ever went my way anymore. First, I wanted to keep my promise to my son and buy him a car, so I did. He ended up picking up an Impala. I didn't like his choice, but he liked that he could call it his own. After some convincing, we traded it in for a different one. Then, Linda told me about a trailer that she saw for sale, and I knew that I had to jump on the opportunity. I contacted the owner and purchased it with the money I had saved from my monthly income, and we moved into the trailer park. We left Linda's house right away, and neither Juwan nor Kimberly complained one bit. Having a place of our own where we wouldn't feel squished or in the way felt pleasing. I had a place to lay my head, and I no longer was homeless. It felt as if we had come full circle by moving back into a trailer. I appreciated everything Linda and Doris did for me during my time of need, but beyond that, nothing changed between us. We went back to taking care of ourselves, and we grew no closer as siblings.

The trailer allowed me to take charge of my life once more and focus on my children's lives and their futures. Kayla and her boyfriend Anthony tied the knot and had two children over the past few years. I loved the fact that I could consider myself a grandfather, and I made sure my daughter knew that she could leave the kids with me any time she needed. I honestly wish they could've stayed with me all the time. I felt determination to provide for them as their grandpa. Kayla ended up having three children total, and I love them all equally.

Juwan and Kayla took care of themselves for the most part during this time. Juwan drove his sister to and from school everyday in his car. Sometimes, they would take my Dodge Stratus instead. They took my car out one day, and my son felt like having some fun. He didn't have a problem with speeding, and a train track sits between the high school and our trailer.

Based on their account after the fact, Juwan said, "Kimberly, I'm going to jump this railroad track."

My daughter replied, "Slow down please." "No, I'm going to jump it."

He floored the gas and didn't let up as the Stratus catapulted over the elevated railroad track and lifted the car several feet off the ground. According to Kimberly, doing so made everything, including the music, cut off. The moment they landed back on the road, it jolted them and the car enough to make it all come back on. The kids told me about it when they got home, and because they caused no damage, I laughed with them as they told me how exhilarating it felt. I just liked the fact that they told me the truth and had some fun.

Kimberly, however, didn't have such luck. She took the Stratus to school one day, and she always loved listening to music on her phone as she did. She had senior pictures at school on this day, so she needed to get there on time. According to my daughter, it happened on one of the curviest roads leading to the school. Someone on an adjacent road turned across traffic on a sharp curve and forced traffic in her lane to stop all of a sudden. Kimberly didn't slam on her brakes quick enough, so she hit the back of the car in front of her. Because my old car had little worth and it had too much damage, we lost the car. Before this point, Kimberly and I had shared the car, and she would drive me to Kayla's house, to various stores, and anywhere else around Greer. I couldn't go anywhere anymore, and Kimberly had to rely on her friends to pick her up for the rest of the school year.

Both my kids graduated high school in their respective years, and I felt proud of their drives to finish school, despite moving from place to place and experiencing everything that I put them through. Juwan worked at a temp agency and took different jobs that changed each day. He moved out and got his own place after saving a little money. Kimberly worked at KFC and Wal-Mart before training for and passing her CNA license exam. She then started to go to school to become a nurse. After everything that I put her through, I also felt proud of the fact that she chose a career centering on helping others. Due to her years of continued schooling, I let her live with me until she determined that she felt that she saved enough money to move out. In exchange, she'd drive me around in her car when she could.

My future nurse daughter suggested that I should go and get a full medical check up done to make sure everything looks good with my physical health. I went to a doctor soon after, and they drew some blood as one of the tests. Kayla and the grandkids came over the next day and answered my phone when the doctor called with the results. She came into the room crying and told me that they learned that I had diabetes and had set me up with a diabetic specialist. I didn't see it as a problem, but both Kayla and Kimberly didn't take it well. They thought that I was dying, but I knew that I was in good shape. To ease their minds, I promised them that I would see my specialist as directed and take steps to stay healthy, including changing my eating habits and exercising more. Daddy had diabetes, so I may have inherited it from him, but then again, I ate quiet a lot of candy and junk food as a kid. Eating poorly could've caused my condition just as well. I began walking around the neighborhood every day. It felt good to get out of the trailer for an hour every day and breathe some fresh air. I eventually quit smoking as well. Because I had also monitored my diet, I ended up losing 20 pounds and bringing my weight down to 175. I found myself in a good place, both mentally and physically.

When I look back at it all, sometimes I wish that my children were still young because at least I had their company to keep me busy and active. If that were the case now, sitting around the trailer wouldn't get so boring, and I wouldn't get so lonely when my grand- children weren't around. If I had a bigger place for them, I could have all my grandkids over at one time. However, I know that I should show appreciation for what I have. Kayla, Juwan, and Kimberly all have families and careers of their own, and I couldn't be prouder. I like to think that I raised them well, despite everything. Though I regret not raising Jonathan, I never left my kids to starve and live in a freezing cold house, as Daddy did.

I look back on my past marriages in an educational light rather than focusing on the negatives. I blame the power company for ruining my first marriage. Because Janice wanted a lot from our marriage but never got a job, so I worked myself to death and tolerated a lot to provide for our family. To this day, Janice and I still get along, and we often get together for cookouts and the like. Despite living in Greer again, I won't let my old coworkers cause me any more stress. As for my second marriage, Lisa wanted money, so she took advantage of my recovery in order to dig her way into my life. Despite my heartbreaks, I look towards finding love again with a hopeful heart. I will take my time with any of my future relationships and get to know my partners well before even considering marriage. I'd like to see if third times the charm.

As for my financials, it took 10 years since the mess in Atlanta to recover my credit. I went from being homeless to living into a trailer to purchasing a brand new, three-bedroom house. I also have a car of my own now that I can take wherever I want. Never will I have to worry about being denied financially ever again. With hard work and perseverance, anything can be accomplished. Turns out, the same can be said about life too.

www.ingramcontent.com/pod-product-compliance
Lightning Source LLC
Chambersburg PA
CBHW020333130626
46549CB00003B/1163